My Dog Kiefer

Trisha Malfitano

K   I   E   F   E   R

Order this book online at www.trafford.com
or email orders@trafford.com

Most Trafford titles are also available at major online book retailers.

Printed in the United States of America.

ISBN: 978-1-4269-6336-0

Library of Congress Control Number: 2011908487

Trafford rev. 05/20/2011

 www.trafford.com

North America & international
toll-free: 1 888 232 4444 (USA & Canada)
phone: 250 383 6864 ♦ fax: 812 355 4082

There is something very special about my dog, Kiefer. He wants to tell you all about himself. See if you can guess what makes Kiefer different from other dogs.

Hi there, as you already know my name is Kiefer. I am a Border Collie. I was adopted from New England Border Collie Rescue. This is the best place in the world if you are a Border Collie that needs to find a new home.

Sister

Form an "a" with your right hand and draw a line along your jawbone from your ear to your chin, then bring both index fingers together to form the sign for "same" - symbolizing a female from the same family.

Brother

Put your right hand to your forehead as if you were holding the rim of a hat between your fingers and your thumb, then move it forward and form the sign for "same" - indicating a male from the same family.

I was born in Rescue with five brothers and two sisters, and we were raised by Grandma Lynn and Auntie Amy. I was only 10 weeks old when I went to my new home. I now live with five other rescue dogs and three cats.

TUG
(struggle)

Point both index fingers at each other and then move them back and forth simultaneously- indicating a tug of war or a struggle.

Here is my real brother, Moss. It is so cool when we get together. We have
so much fun playing different games. Our favorite game is tug. We each take
an end of the tug toy and just run and run and run. If you come outside
with us you need to watch out, we can't steer very well.

CHASE

Place both "a" hands in front of you with your left hand in front of your right hand slightly, then move them forward with your right hand rapidly chasing after your left hand.

Play, play, play. I love to play. When I am not visiting Moss, I have friends at home I can play with. Can you believe one of my best friends is a cat? Tabasco and I wrestle and play chase. When we play chase, he runs and I run after him.

WATER

With a "w" hand, touch
your index finger to your
mouth a few times as if
you are bringing a drink of
water to your mouth.

Playing outside is fun. When it gets really hot outside my brother, Phoenix, and I like to play with the hose. We are very silly. While Alex holds the hose, we bark and bite at the water coming out. When we are all done, we are soaking wet.

WALK

Using your down turned index and middle finger, make a forward walking motion.

I also love to go on walks with Nikki. They are mini adventures. I am always sniffing the ground and looking at everything. On windy days I can chase leaves as they blow across the street. It's always great when I get to meet new people. They always say how cute I am.

SECRET

Place the "a" hand over your sealed lips several times indicating that your lips are sealed tight.

Have you guessed what's so special about Kiefer? If you know, keep it a secret for now. Some people might not know yet.

SIT

Form the letter "h" with both hands, then place the right "h" on top of the left "h" and move both hands down symbolizing a person sitting down on a chair.

Did you know that I am a very smart dog? I went to obedience school. I learned how to sit, lie down, and come when asked. If I want extra treats I have to sit very still and not jump on people. Mom is trying to teach me how to roll over; we still need a lot of practice.

BATH

Move both "a" hands up and down in front of your chest a few times illustrating washing your body.

There are so many things that I love but there is one thing I don`t like at all... BATH TIME! I like getting all wet, but I would rather go roll in the dirt than get covered in bubbles. Look how silly I look all clean. YUCK.

PLAY

Pivot both "y" hands in front of your chest several times, symbolizing hands that are free to play.

On some days the other dogs don't want to play with me. When this happens I play by myself. I like to throw my toys in the air and try to catch them. Sometimes I just run up and down the hall hoping someone will join in.

GOOD

Put your right hand up to your mouth, then move the hand down into the open palm of your left hand with both palms facing up indicating that you have tasted something good so you are passing it on to share with someone else.

I enjoy visiting different places. Once I went to pre-school to visit my good friend, Kyley. She wanted to show me to all her friends. The kids asked all sorts of questions about me. I was such a good boy. I got lots of hugs and pats on the head.

CLIMB

Shape both hands into a curved "v" facing one another and make alternating climbing motions with each hand similar to climbing a rope or a ladder.

Once I got to go hiking. I really enjoyed climbing up the rocks and exploring in the bushes. My buddy, Gavin, came with me. He likes to go hiking, too. I was very proud of myself when I made it all the way to the top of the mountain. I hope to go again and maybe climb higher.

I LOVE YOU

Hold up your right hand, palm facing forward with the little finger, index finger, and thumb extended, combining the letters "i", "l", and "y" to form I Love You.

At night time I sleep in a crate. It has a warm blanket and my favorite pillow for me to sleep on. I also get a treat when I go into my crate all by myself. Mommy always says "Good night" and "I love you" to all of us dogs.

KISS

Place the fingers of your right hand on your mouth and then move them up to your cheek suggesting two common places to be kissed.

The best part of sleeping in the crate is the morning. As soon as you let me out, I jump all around and give tons of kisses to anyone who is around. I give the best doggy kisses in the world.

DEAF

Point to your right ear with your right index finger, then bring both hands together and form the sign for "closed".

So did you guess yet? If you guessed that Kiefer is deaf, you are right.
Kiefer was born deaf. I have to use my hands to talk to him. As you already
know, Kiefer can do everything a hearing dog can do. Kiefer doesn't know that
he is different, and he isn't sad about it.

I hope to learn lots of new things to say with my hands so I can keep teaching Kiefer new things. Remember, if you ever meet a deaf dog, just use your hands instead of your voice to say hello.

Trisha has always had a passion for animals. She has also always enjoyed reading to her children. This book was created out of her love from both. She now shares her home with her husband, two girls, 6 rescue dogs and 3 rescue cats.

* * * * * * * * * * * * * * * * * *

Have you ever known someone who was made fun of because they were different? Maybe you have a family member or friend who others consider "special". Do they get treated fairly? I have gone to school with people who the world considered unworthy because they had physical problems or problems learning like the rest of the class. I recently had the privilege of working with a special needs child. I have learned so much about the kind of person I want to be from this experience. I could never understand why people are not more excepting of others who are different. Last year I adopted a puppy who was born deaf. I could not believe how many people thought he was not worth saving because he is deaf. This book is for all the people and animals that the world has tossed aside as not good enough. All life is beautiful and should be treated as such.

Printed by
EDWARDS BROTHERS
www.edwardsbrothers.com
07SKC11MDJa